TEDDY
THE SPAZ MAN

A funny dog
with a
million expressions

Designed by Diane Reyerson-Warren

ISBN # 978-0-9994666-0-5

First Edition: October 2017

This book is dedicated to Roxie Love.
She was my mentor, my rock, my everything.
We love you and miss you more than we can say.

Table of Contents

laugh

Teddy the Spaz Man

pee your fur pants

fart nugget

Mr. Johnson

hound hole

daisy dukes

she-dogs

Acknowledgements

To my husband Aaron, thank you for your ridiculous amount of support and patience through this journey with Teddy. Who knew a Facebook page created on a whim would lead to his very own book? A book! You've been there through it all, getting hammered with endless questions like, "Is this funny? What if I use this word? What about this pic? Oh no, you didn't laugh, I'll keep working on it." Even though your eyes glazed over a few times, you always listened and even threw out some great suggestions! And thank you for helping with the countless photo shoots. You are the best photography assistant ever!

Mom and Dad, as your daughter, I want to thank you for always giving me the freedom to be exactly who I am. If you hadn't laughed at all my jokes, goofy faces and crazy leg kicks, I might've ended up a doctor in some big hospital where I would go on to save thousands of SQUIRREL! — Ha ha! See? THAT'S why I appreciate you so much. You recognized and encouraged MY gifts and that is the best gift of all. Thank you!

Thanks to my family and friends. I couldn't ask for a more supportive bunch. You've all heard your fair share of quips and ideas, usually in the form of a frantic phone call. "You think this is funny? Yeah? Ok, thanks, bye!" You guys always root me on and give me your honest opinions, which I appreciate so much.

To Teddy's social media fans, you guys are amazing! Without you, I'd still be sitting in my closet, feverishly scribbling funnies and cackling like a hyena all by myself. Through Teddy, you've given me an outlet to share my creativity and I'm so thankful.

I also want to thank you for being a part of our lives. You brighten our days with your hilarious comments, soothe our hearts with your compassion and you've helped build a supportive, loving community of fellow animal lovers. That's huge and we're so very grateful.

And finally, I'd like to thank you, Teddy. The way you came into our lives is much like so many others have experienced. A beloved fur baby passes and you crave that energy again so you go in search of a new friend.

Thank you for renewing our spirits after our sweet Buddy Boy passed. You and your fur siblings mean the world to your dad and me, and we're honored to share our lives with you. To think someone tied you to a post, discarding you like trash is beyond comprehension. I'm so sorry you had to go through that. One man's "trash", you are our treasure. My wish is that no animal will ever feel as though they're not wanted or that they're not the most precious creature on earth.

Introduction

This is a photo book about a dog named Teddy. He's a hound who dates saucy little she-dogs, plays endless pranks on his nemesis neighbor Mr. Johnson, and is more dude than dog. He loves to travel, shop, hike and dine at the finest fur-star restaurants.

Teddy's astute observations on everyday situations make him not only relatable but hilarious — probably 'cause he says what most of us think!

He could probably use a lesson in modesty because his ego is a little on the, uh, healthy side.

So come along and laugh, gasp and shake your head at Teddy's crazy, never-ending antics. I double dog dare you not to fall in love!

While Teddy loves his outdoor adventures, he is by no means an outside dog. No siree Bob! Like every pet we've ever had, he likes his air conditioning and the comforts of a nice, big bed. He loves to snuggle too, so most nights are spent curled up on the couch either next to my husband and me or next to his furry siblings, who you'll get to meet later in the book.

To think that meeting him would lead me to write a book is nuts, especially since this all happened so innocently. Like any proud mom, I showed him off on my personal Facebook profile and after my friends saw his funny faces, they encouraged me to start a Facebook page for him. I thought, what the heck, it'll be a good way to entertain my friends without cluttering their newsfeeds.

From the very first post, Teddy did his own talking, which just seemed natural since he's half dude. I invited some of my friends to like his page and from there, it just kind of snowballed. Next thing I knew, he had thousands of friends from all over the world!

I figured he'd provide a few chuckles so it shocked me when I began receiving messages from his fans telling me that he not only made them laugh but he helped them get through some rough times. Whether it was the loss of their pet, dealing with an illness, or they had just gone through a breakup, they let me know that Teddy's humor and crazy antics helped them forget their troubles for a minute. That was powerful stuff.

Realizing Teddy had this effect on people gave me a newfound purpose, and in a strange way, I felt a responsibility to introduce him to as many people as possible. I mean, if he had that kind of effect on just his fans who wrote me, he could potentially save the world! Ha! Ok, I'm joking, but seriously, laughter and feeling good is contagious and the world needs more of it so if Teddy and I can help spread even a little of that, then sign us up!

Oh, and about his name! I get asked all the time about how his name came to be, so here it is. The folks at the shelter named him Teddy and we thought it fit him so we kept that. The Spaz Man wasn't planned, it just came naturally about five minutes after he was in our house. His crazy energy and Gumby-like body moved so fast and furiously, that it was hard to keep up. Then in the middle of tearing around, he'd stop and look at us with this funny grin, like he was waiting for a reaction. He KNEW he was funny and it cracked us up. I was affectionately called 'Spaz' as a kid and it always made me stand a little taller because I knew I was making someone laugh. And that's exactly how I saw Teddy.

Then

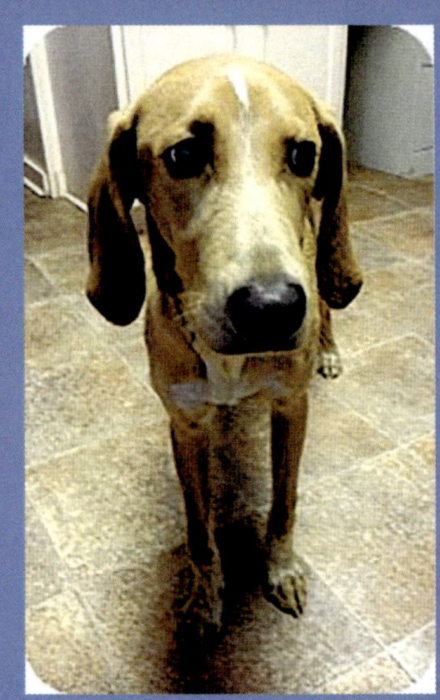

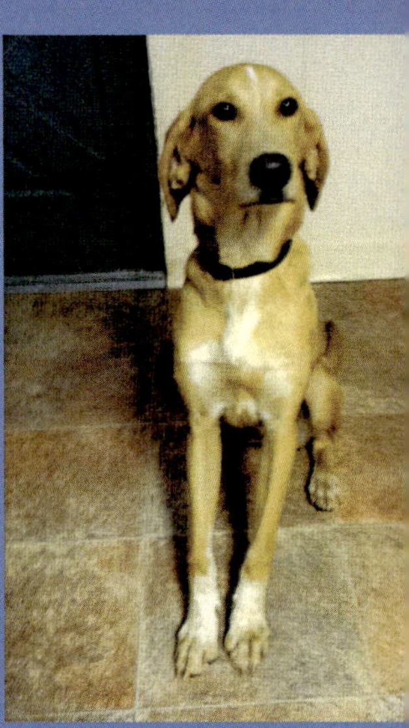

The awesome volunteers
at Big Canoe Animal Rescue found me
tied up outside their shelter one morning.
They took me in, cared for me and
helped me find my forever home.

Now

To the people who
abandoned me, I say,
"Look at me now, fart nuggets!"

Laughter is the Best Medicine

Wait, is bacon medicine?

Dad was lookin' for
the controller so I said,
"I think she's in the kitchen!"

You sure you are
what you eat?
'Cause I don't remember
eatin' a sexy beast.

You think I wanna bite
of your sandwich?
Don't be ridiculous.
I want the whole thing.

Nope, I'm not muggin' for
the camera 'til you take this
ridiculous thing off my head.

I might have to go to
obedience school.

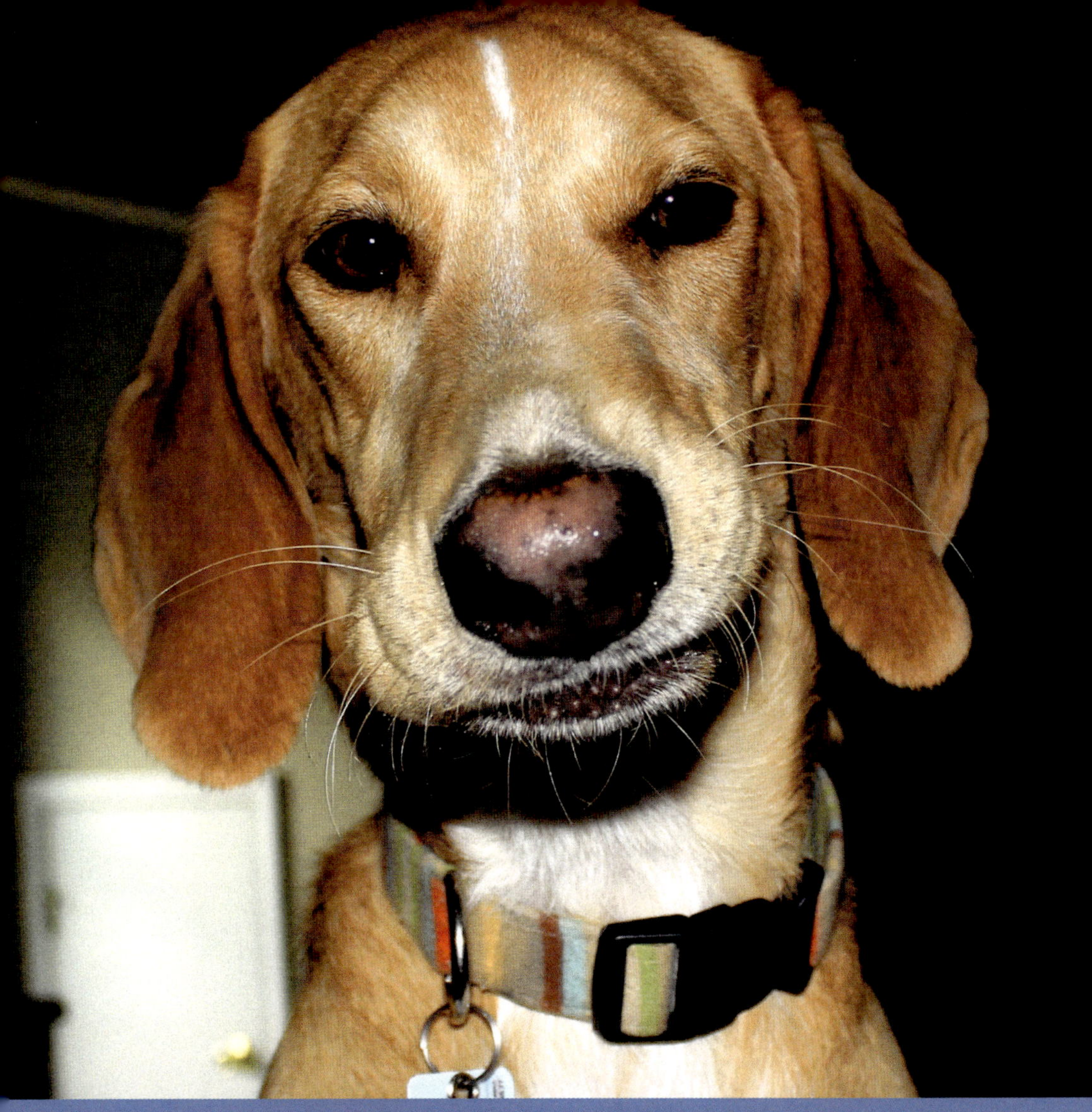

She looks so peaceful
layin' there sleeping.
I may have to howl.

Mom wanted to do
a streaming video
so I started peeing.

When someone
calls me out for
swipin' their food.

Did I steal your cake?
I can't answer that.
You told me not to talk
with my mouth full.

Say hello to
my weapon of
sass destruction.

Played tug-o'-war.
With dad's underwear.
While he was on the toilet.

Eatin' one of
mom's cookies.
Betty Crocker she's not.

Dad just explained neutering.
#nightmares

I poke holes
in poop bags.

Dear God, please
let me pass the cat
on the stairs today
without peeing myself.

Ready for my close-up.

I'm the flappiest
dog in the whole
wide world!

I love to lose myself in
interpretive dance. I call this,
'The Wind Beneath My Ears'.

Dad said he
better not see ONE more
turd in the house. I was like,
"Well then ya better stay
away from the mirrors."

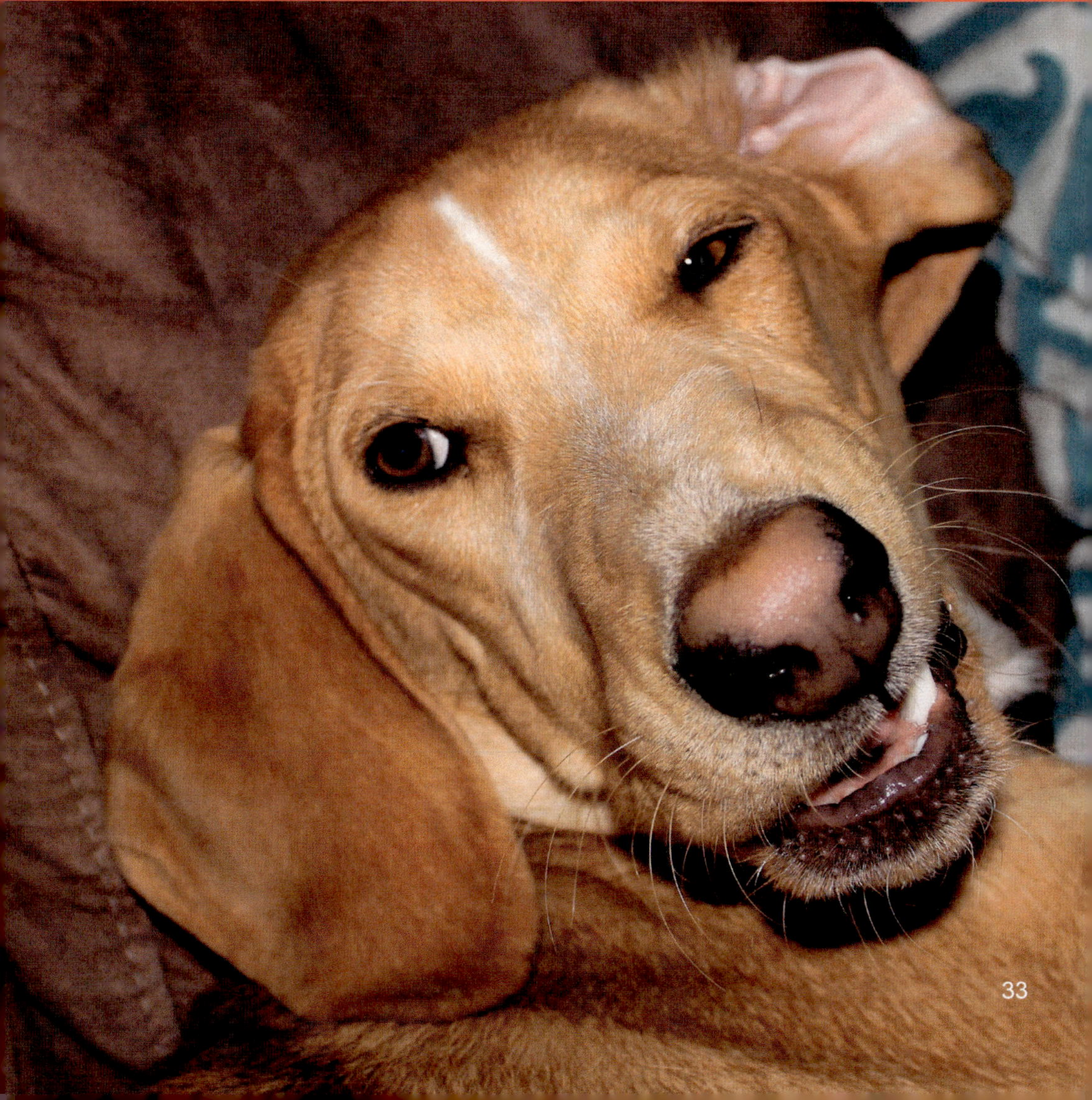

I was in a spelling bee
and the word was handsome.
I answered, "Handsome.
T.E.D.D.Y. Handsome."

You said if I smiled pretty,
you'd gimme some sugar.
I'll take it sprinkled on
a bacon donut, please.

I just love sitting in
my sun-dappled yard.
Oops, darn auto correct.
Sitting is missing a letter.

When I'm in
MY house and someone
tells me to stop barking!

Hey dad,
the doc called and said he
messed up mom's vocal cords so she
won't be able to talk for a week. You think
flowers would be nice or should we just
send him a thank you card?

The aliens are comin'!
No anal probes.
NO ANAL PROBES!

I am NOT gonna apologize
for diggin' those holes.
Now I'm gonna run like the wind.

I was out for a stroll
when a woman said she liked
my bow tie AND halter top.
I didn't even try to hide my disdain.

42

Meet My Family

A mixed bag
of whackadoos

Family is everything. They help shape who we are, teach us things, and make us laugh even when we don't feel like it – and my family's no exception, which is why I want you to meet everyone.

A few have gone on to the Rainbow Bridge since I was adopted in September 2014, but they've all been, and continue to be, a very important part of my life.

Before losing Roxie Love, Lucille and Sydney, there were six of us furry and feathered babies living under the same roof. It just goes to show that animals of different breeds, sizes, genders, and even species, can not only get along, but actually like each other!

Oh, and ya know how they say hounds and cats don't mix? Well I have no idea what they're talkin' about because I hit it off with my sister cats right from the start.

Buddy & Jack
The two originals. Buddy was the
sweetest soul ever and Jack was
mom's first heart dog.

Roxie Love
Mom's soul sister and my everything.
Smart, confident,
compassionate and oh-so funny.

Mama Kitty
Always ready to box
someone's ears in.

Lucille
Cool, calm
and so loving.

Sydney
Bossy, sassy and smarter
than all of us put together.

Yogi
A foster failure tripawd who went
from bitter biter to total love bug.

Violet Willow aka Kudzu
The goofiest little
runt I've ever met.

Mom
She's pretty cool. After all, I tell her
what to write and she does it.
She takes my pics too.
And hugs me. Like a lot.

Dad
He's the kinda guy who'll stop traffic
to save an animal. ANY animal.
And he shares his cheese curds.
I think I'll keep him.

Family Funnies

A fur-flyin'
frenzy of fun!

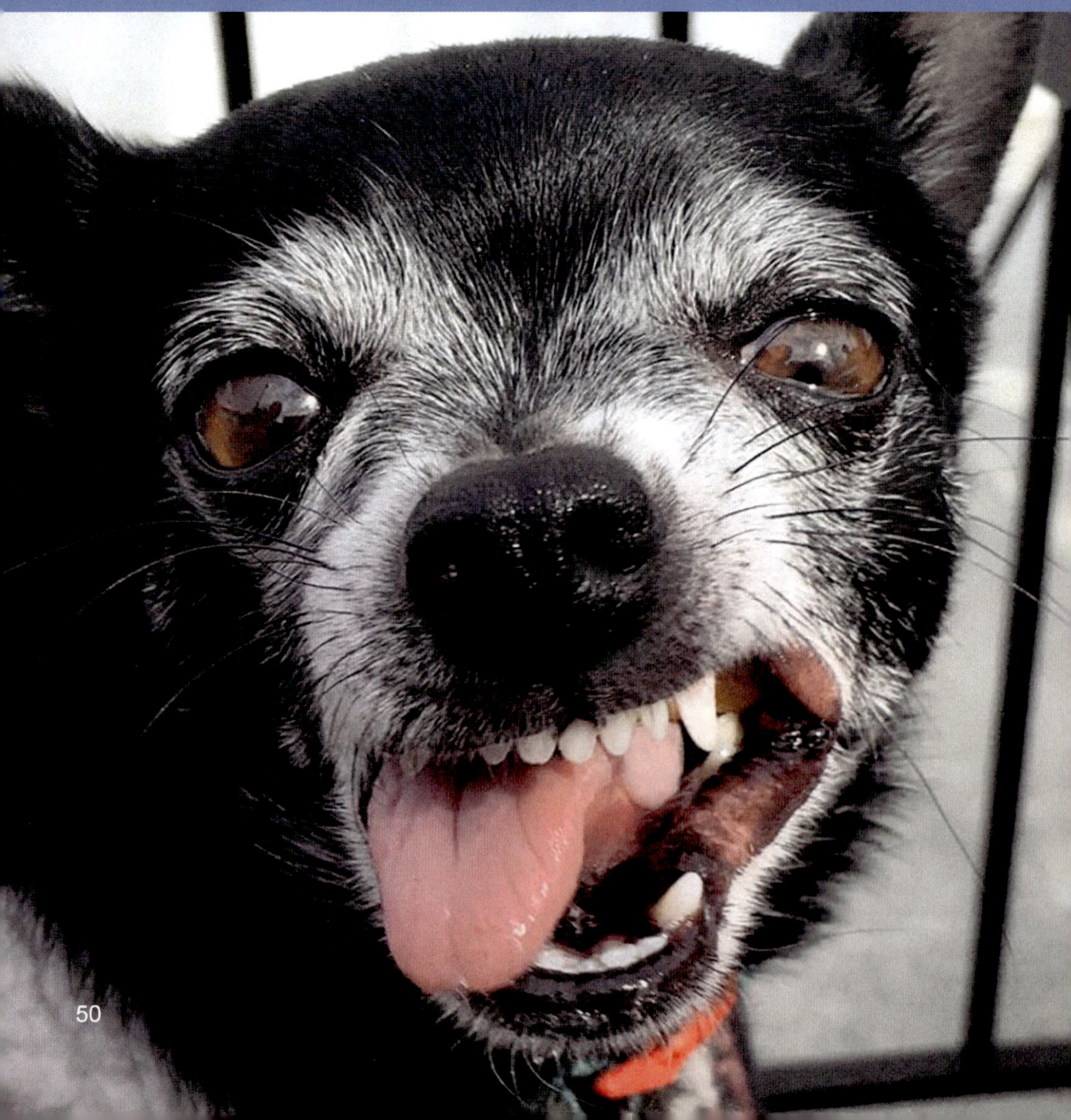

I told Yogi to clean
the litter box. He doesn't do
well with authority.

Daaaaaaad!

I should tell Violet to stop diggin' that hole but why ruin such EXCELLENT blackmail material.

Takin' Mama Kitty
to the Annual Hair Ball.
I see she's practicing.

53

Violet

I swear she was
born with a feather up her
rumpasaurous. She thinks
EVERYTHING is funny.

I know Violet,
I love you too.

Yogi got his "senior" pictures taken.

I convinced Violet
she was lactose intolerant
so I could have her
cheese puffs.

Walking Small
on yard patrol.

There's somethin'
not quite right
with this one.

Sydney and Mama Kitty
holding one of their
secret meetings.
No doubt plotting to
take over the world.

Oh goody, it's time for
the backyard ballet
with Mr. Tinkle Toes.

Mr. Johnson

My neighbor from
H.E. double hockey sticks

My Neighbor and #1 Nemesis

Ahh, good ole Mr. Johnson. He first caught my eye when he was struttin' around in his halter top and daisy dukes. He's (ahem) a tad bit eccentric and completely obsessed with me. He lives next door and watches me in the backyard from his upstairs bedroom window. I can't make a move without his beady eyes trackin' me!

And get this! He even faked his own death one time so I'd give him mouth-to-mouth (hold on while I throw up a little).

Ok, I'm back.

Yeah, so even though I'm a pretty easy goin' dude, there comes a time in every dog's life when you just have to put your paw down and say enough is enough. That time has come!!!

Got my disguise on
so I can spy on Mr. Johnson.
There's some freaky stuff
goin' on over there.

I felt bad being mean
to Mr. Johnson every time
he opened his mouth so I ran over
and slapped a muzzle on him.

Mr. Johnson's sportin' a tutu.
My corneas are scorched.

I just gave
Mr. Johnson a brand new,
fully loaded poop bag!

Aaagh!
Mr. Johnson's bendin' over
prunin' his rose bushes!
I saw his elderberries!!!

You Gotta Be Kiddin' Me

I was leavin' with my date when Mr. Johnson yelled down, "Hey little lady, did Teddy here tell ya he wants ten kids?"

She gasped and hightailed it as fast as she could. I chased after her yelling, "Not those kinda kids! Goats! I want ten GOATS!!!"

But she was gone, and all that remained was the maniacal laughter of Mr. Johnson.

I had flowers delivered to
Mr. Johnson for his birthday.
I heard poison ivy's his favorite!

Sometimes I just
sit in the backyard and make
faces at Mr. Johnson all day.
Don't judge, you have
your job, I have mine.

Mr. Johnson
needed gas money
so I ran over and
farted in his wallet.

Waiting for
Mr. Johnson to eat the
cream-filled donuts I made him.
Hope he likes mayonnaise.

73

She-Dogs

Tall, short,
thin, chunky
black, brown,
white, brindle,
bug-eyed,
stink-eyed,
I love 'em all!

How YOU doin'?

Sometimes I just hang by my truck and let the she-dogs admire me. It's my way of giving back.

Great, my date's here
and I got a serious case of
erect tail dysfunction.

When you wanna smooch but the cute little Shih Tzu thinks you're making fun of her underbite.

When your date's
a gluten-free, flavor-free,
fun-free vegan.

Dreamin' I'm bein'
fed bacon-wrapped donuts
by a harem of Poodles.
Don't wake me.

A saucy little she-dog
said I was houndsome
and I was like,
"Who, meeee?"

My ex just walked by like
she's all that and a bag of chips.
She's a bag of chips alright.
A bag of BUFFALO chips.

Showin' off my
super smooth dance moves
for the she-dogs.

Stop!

I'm gonna pee
my fur pants!

Saw a dude trip.
Laughed so hard I snorted.

When your boss sends
you a friend request.

Nope, no one's
leavin' this house
'til I see a leash.

I was kinda razzin'
this guy for talkin' outta the corner
of his mouth. Finally, dad said if I kept it
up the guy was gonna gimme a knuckle
sandwich. Naturally, I cranked it up a
notch 'cause I've never had one
but a knuckle sandwich
sounds delicious!

Knock knock.
Who's there?
Madame.
Madame who?
Madame tongue keeps fallin' out.

Jumped on dad this morning
'cause he was gonna be late
for work. Forgot it was Saturday.
I felt HORRIBLE.
So I did it again.

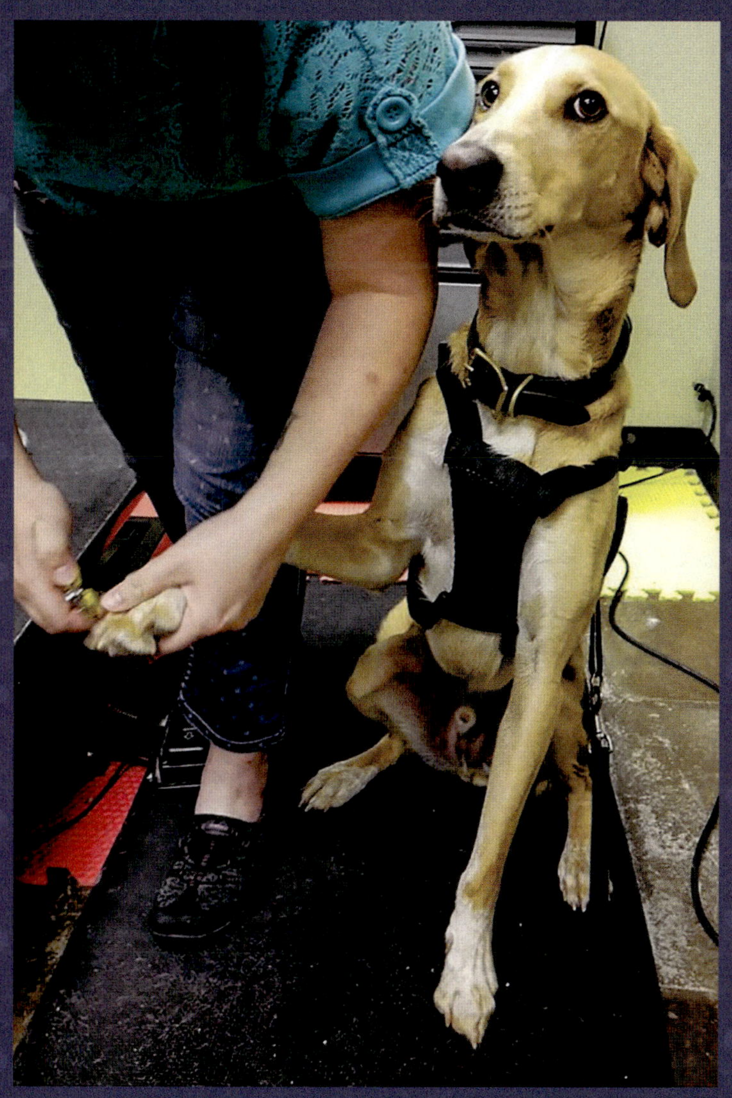

I'm letting her trim
'em but if she whips out
the nail polish I'm biting
all of you.

Dog?
I prefer the term
Furry Bad Butt.

It's bath day
so I wore my camos.
Those fools'll
never find me.

The ice cream truck
drove right past by me!
Wait 'til he gets a load
of MY soft serve!

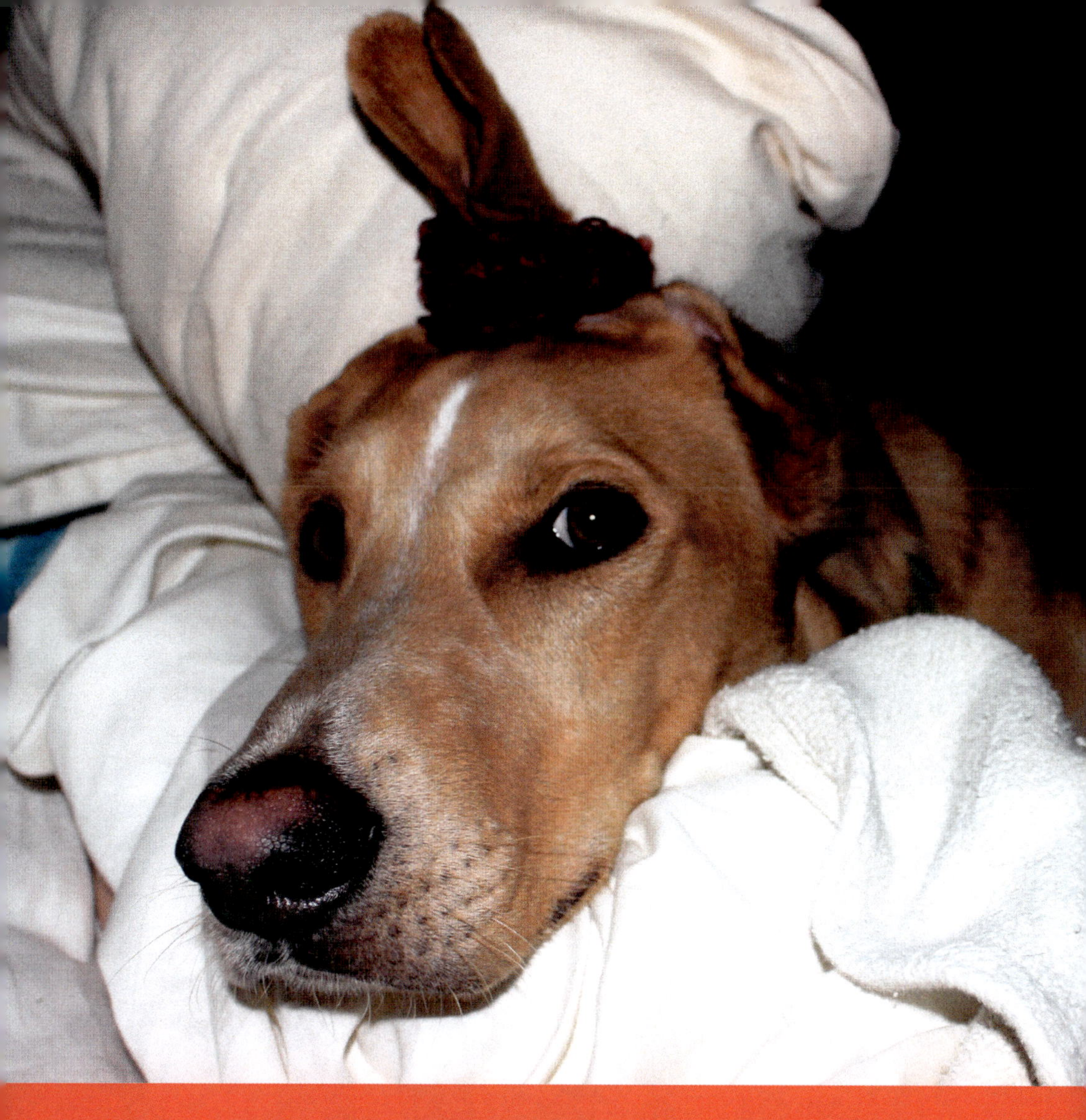

Yeah, I wear a
scrunchie to bed.
And?

Someone call the
houndsome police
'cause I'm killin' it.

They call me Damus.
NOSTRIL Damus.

Oh, so your "me time" is more important than my bedtime story? I'll remember that when YOU wanna snuggle!

98

I tripped my vet as he
was leavin' the store and his
stuff went flyin' everywhere.
I was like, "Ha! Now we
BOTH have empty sacks!"

Sometimes I just
sit super still and smile.
Freaks people out.

Dad was gonna take my
stuffie so I kicked up my heels,
yelled "No way man!"
and shot him an air biscuit.

Ok friend,
that's all she wrote!
Hope you loved my book!

And remember, I LOVE talkin' to my
fans online so come by and say hi!

facebook.com/teddythespazman
instagram.com/teddythespazman

Made in the USA
Columbia, SC
12 June 2021

39967928R00060